MOUNTAINS AROUND THE WORLD

The Urals

By Robin Johnson

Crabtree Publishing Company

www.crabtreebooks.com

Crabtree Publishing Company

www.crabtreebooks.com

Author: Robin Johnson
Editor: Adrianna Morganelli
Proofreader: Kathy Middleton
Indexer: Wendy Scavuzzo
Designer: Katherine Berti
Photo researchers:
Katherine Berti & Crystal Sikkens
Project coordinator: Kathy Middleton
Production coordinator & prepress technician: Katherine Berti

Front cover: Unique rock formations can be seen in the Nether-polar Urals in West Siberia.

Title page: This forest in the Urals is brightly colored with autumn leaves.

Pictures credits:
Katherine Berti: p. 21
Corbis: © Serguei Fomine/GlobalLook: p. 23 (top right); © Wolfgang Kaehler: p. 41 (top)
Dreamstime: p. 27 (top), 39 (bottom)
iStockphoto: p. 17 (top), 20 (top)
Keystone Press: Zumapress: p. 13, 15 (bottom)
Samara Parent: p. 5
Shutterstock: p. 1, 4, 6, 7 (top and middle), 8, 9 (top), 10, 11 (bottom), 14 (bottom right), 15 (top), 16, 17 (bottom), 18, 19, 20 (bottom), 22, 23 (top left and bottom), 24 (bottom), 25, 26, 27 (bottom), 28, 30, 31 (bottom left and bottom right), 32, 33 (top left and bottom), 34, 36, 37, 38 (bottom), 40, 41 (bottom), 42, 43, 44, 45
Wikimedia Commons: Ugraland: p. 7 (bottom); Yamigos: p. 9 (bottom); Wikigraphist: p. 11 (top); Godfrey Kneller: p. 12; Bernt Rostad: p. 14 (top); Ds02006: p. 14 (bottom left); Acodered: p. 24 (top); Alex Bakharev: p. 29 (top); www.globalconnections.co.uk/: p. 29 (bottom); Xviona: p. 31 (top); Latitude: p. 33 (top right); Bridget Samuels: p. 35 (left); Francis Larrede: p. 35 (right); DVS: p. 38 (top); Ecodefense/ Heinrich Boell Stiftung Russia/Slapovskaya/ Nikulina: p. 39 (top)

Library and Archives Canada Cataloguing in Publication

Johnson, Robin (Robin R.)
The Urals / Robin Johnson.

(Mountains around the world)
Includes index.
Issued also in electronic formats.
ISBN 978-0-7787-7564-5 (bound).--ISBN 978-0-7787-7571-3 (pbk.)

1. Ural Mountains (Russia)--Juvenile literature. 2. Ural Mountains Region (Russia)--Juvenile literature. I. Title. II. Series: Mountains around the world (St. Catharines, Ont.)

DK511.U7J64 2011 j914.7'43 C2011-905226-1

Library of Congress Cataloging-in-Publication Data

Johnson, Robin (Robin R.)
The Urals / Robin Johnson.
p. cm. -- (Mountains around the world)
Includes index.
ISBN 978-0-7787-7564-5 (reinforced library binding : alk. paper) -- ISBN 978-0-7787-7571-3 (pbk. : alk. paper) -- ISBN 978-1-4271-8845-8 (electronic PDF) -- ISBN 978-1-4271-9748-1 (electronic HTML)
1. Natural history--Russia (Federation)--Ural Mountains--Juvenile literature. 2. Ural Mountains (Russia)--History--Juvenile literature. 3. Ural Mountains (Russia)--Environmental conditions--Juvenile literature. 4. Mountain life--Russia (Federation)--Ural Mountains--Juvenile literature. I. Title. II. Series.

QH161.J64 2012
947'.43--dc23

2011029827

Crabtree Publishing Company

www.crabtreebooks.com 1-800-387-7650

Printed in Canada/092011/MA20110714

 In Canada: We acknowledge the financial support of the Government of Canada through the Canada Book Fund for our publishing activities.

Published in Canada
Crabtree Publishing
616 Welland Ave.
St. Catharines, Ontario
L2M 5V6

Published in the United States
Crabtree Publishing
PMB 59051
350 Fifth Avenue, 59th Floor
New York, New York 10118

Published in the United Kingdom
Crabtree Publishing
Maritime House
Basin Road North, Hove
BN41 1WR

Published in Australia
Crabtree Publishing
3 Charles Street
Coburg North
VIC 30

CONTENTS

Words that are defined in the glossary are in **bold** type the first time they appear in the text.

CHAPTER 1

The Great Divide

The Ural Mountains are a long, winding mountain range that splits Russia between the continents of Europe and Asia. They are one of the oldest mountain ranges in the world. They formed 250 to 300 million years ago. The Ural Mountains are also one of the lowest mountain ranges on Earth. Only a few peaks in the range are higher than 4,000 feet (1,200 m). Although that may seem high—especially when you are climbing them—they are considered low for a mountain range.

Long ago, Russians called the Ural Mountains the "Stone Belt" because it was a rocky, narrow strip of land dividing the continents of Europe and Asia.

What is a Mountain?

A mountain is a gigantic natural landform that rises above Earth's surface. A mountain often has steep sides rising to a summit, which is the highest point or peak. Mountains are usually found in long ranges or groups of ranges called chains. They are formed in different ways, but most of the mountains on Earth have formed over millions of years. You may not be able to notice or feel it, but mountains are forming even as you read this book!

The climate of the Urals can be severe, with long, freezing winters and short summers. Despite the harsh weather, a variety of plants and animals live on the slopes of the low mountains. **Indigenous** people also traveled and settled throughout the mountains for thousands of years. They depended on the numerous **natural resources** of the Urals for their survival. Over the last century, the Ural Mountains have become an important center of industry for Russia. Mining and manufacturing are big businesses in the Urals. Tourism is also a growing industry, as travelers from around the world begin to discover the hidden gems of the Ural Mountains.

NOTABLE QUOTE

"The Urals are the country's backbone, its main supplier and blacksmith, a region as old as Russia's glory, and the maker of its present-day glory."

—Russian poet Alexander Tvardovsky

High Five

The Ural Mountains run north to south and form a natural boundary between Europe and Asia. The mountain range is about 1,550 miles (2,500 km) long. It stretches from the Kara Sea, which is part of the Arctic Ocean, in northern Russia down to the Ural River in Kazakhstan. The two islands off the mainland in the north are also considered extensions of the Urals. **Geographers** divide this large land area into five sections: the Polar, Nether-Polar, Northern, Central, and Southern Urals. Each area of the Urals has different landforms, weather, plants, animals, resources, and other features.

In the Ural Mountains, tourists can visit two continents at the same time! A monument near the city of Yekaterinburg marks the border between Europe and Asia. Visitors to the site can straddle the line and stand with one foot in each continent!

There are fewer forests in the Polar Urals than in other parts. The land is sparsely covered with swamps, bogs, trees, shrubs, and lichens.

Polar Urals

The Polar Urals make up the narrow northernmost part of the mountain range. This area is also called the Arctic Urals. Mountains here stretch from Mount Konstantinov Kamen in the north to the Khulga River in the south. Some of the mountains in the Polar Urals have sharp peaks and ridges, while others are flat or rounded. Most mountains are about 3,300 feet (1,000 m) or more above sea level.

Many river valleys are found among the mountains in the Nether-Polar Urals.

Nether-Polar Urals

Moving south, the next area of the Ural Mountains is the Nether-Polar area. It is also called the Sub-Arctic or Pre-Polar area. It stretches down to the Shchugor River. Here, the mountain range is wider and the peaks are higher than in the Polar Urals. In fact, the highest mountains of the range—Mount Narodnaya, Mount Karpinsky, and Manaraga—are found in the Nether-Polar area. The mountains are jagged and are split by river valleys.

Manaraga is one of the most well-known mountains in the Urals. Its jagged peaks have earned it the nickname "Bear's Paw."

Northern Urals

The Northern Urals are in the middle of the mountain range. They stretch south to the Usa River. These mountains reach about the same heights as the mountains in the Polar Urals. Most of the **summits** in this area have been flattened by nature over time, however.

The mountain slopes and summits within the Northern Urals have been shaped by erosion.

People's Mountain

The tallest peak in the Urals is Mount Narodnaya in the Nether-Polar region. It is about 6,217 feet (1,895 m) high. Discovered in 1927 by an expedition of scientists, it was named *Narodnaya*, which means "People's Mountain," to honor the people of Russia.

The Chusovaya River begins on the eastern slopes of the Urals in Asia, crosses the mountains, and ends on the western slopes in Europe.

Central Urals

The Central Urals continue the range down to the Ufa River. This area has the lowest mountains of the entire range. There are very few high peaks in this part of the Urals. Instead, it is made up of low hills that have become smooth and rounded over time. The hills of the Central Urals are also dotted with rocks in some places.

Southern Urals

The Southern Urals are made up of high, flat ridges and valleys. They make up the widest and southernmost part of the mountain range. The area extends south to the Ural River. There, the mountains roll into the **uplands** of the Mughalzhar Hills, a series of mountain ranges in northwestern Kazakhstan.

At 5,381 feet (1,640 m), Mount Yamantau is the highest mountain in the Southern Urals.

CHAPTER 2

Geography of the Urals

The Ural Mountains formed millions of year ago when layers of rock on the Earth's surface were pushed together. The layers bent and folded and were pushed upward over time to form tall mountains. Mountains that are formed in this way are called fold or folded mountains. They are the most common type of mountain. The Alps, Andes, Rockies, and other large mountain ranges around the world are also fold mountains.

There are many incredible rock formations, called *boitsy*, along the Chusovaya River.

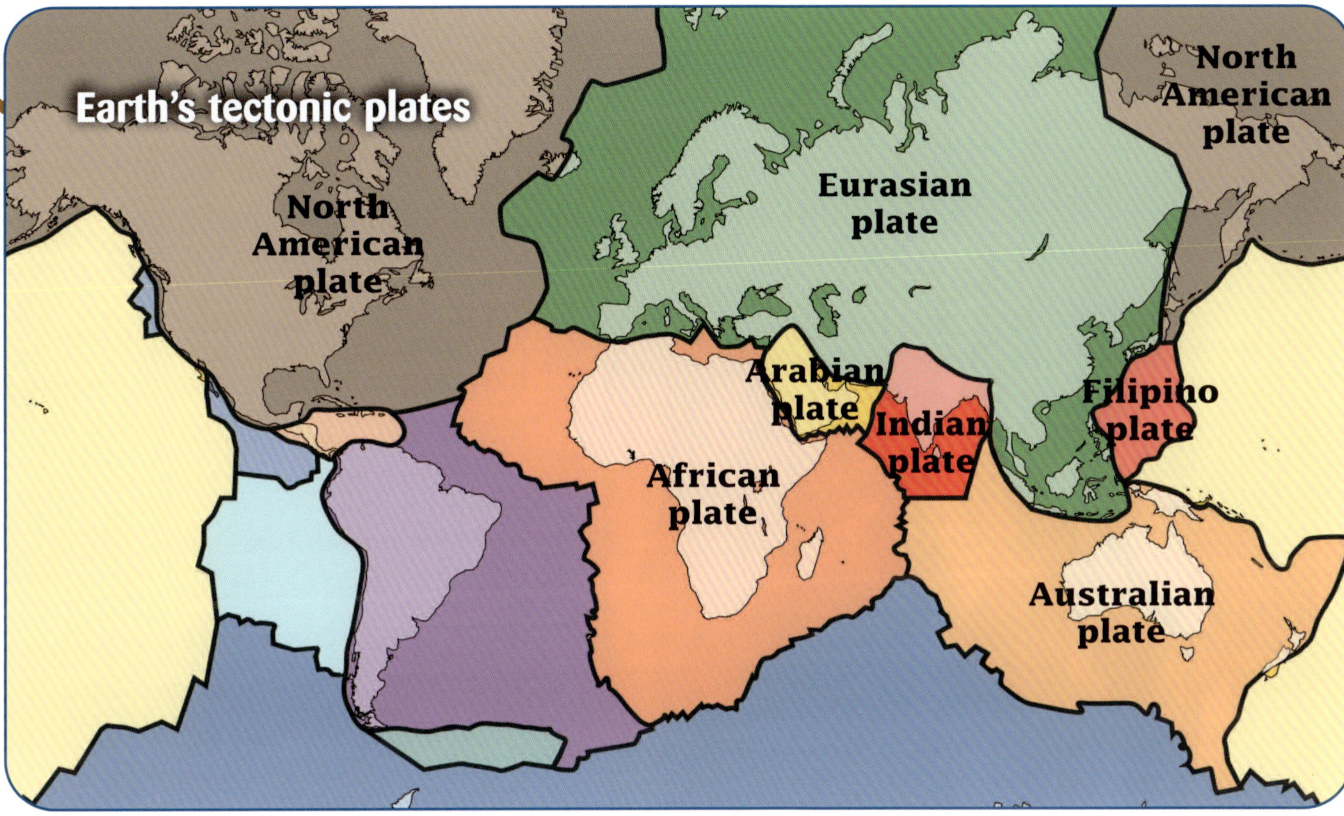

When Worlds Collide

The surface of Earth is made up of huge pieces of floating land called tectonic plates. The plates fit together like giant puzzle pieces. Sometimes, the plates move slowly together or apart. When that happens, the shape of the Earth changes. Millions of years ago, the continents of Europe and Asia were on separate tectonic plates. When the plates collided, their edges joined together and pushed up to form the Ural Mountains. The new tectonic plate became the Eurasian plate.

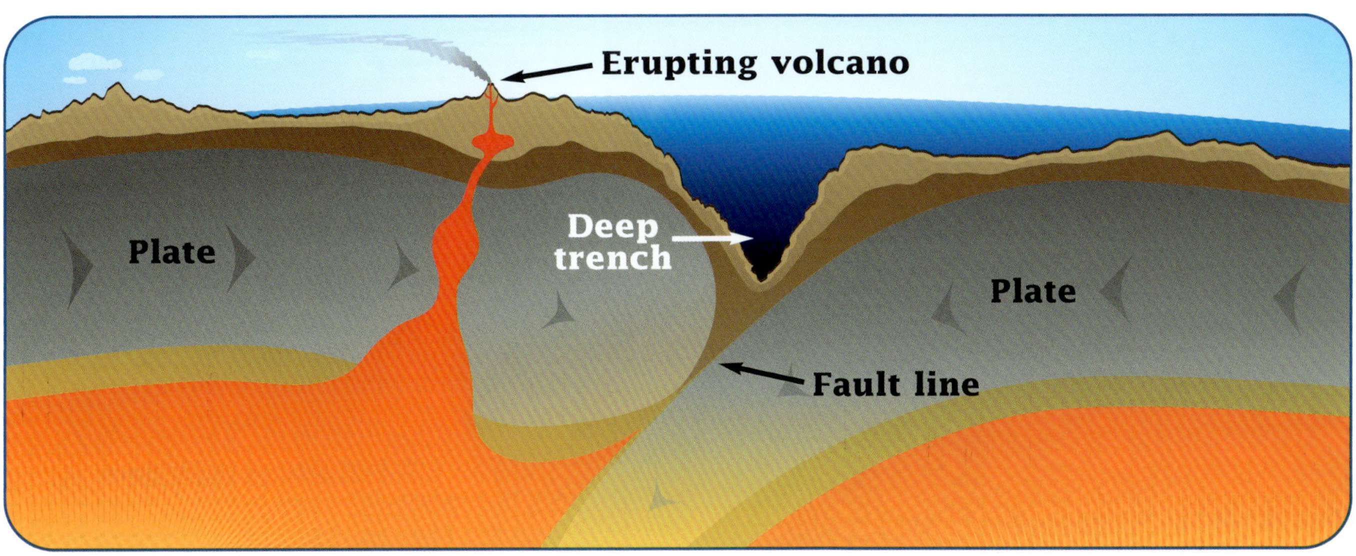

In the early 1700s, Tsar Peter I, known as Peter the Great, ordered the first **survey** of the Ural Mountains.

Eroding Mountains

Long ago, the Urals were very high mountains. They were tall and pointed like the Alps and Himalayas. In fact, scientists believe the Urals may have been some of the highest mountains in the world. Today, the Urals are low mountains because they have been affected by millions of years of **erosion**. Wind, rivers, rain, snow, and ice continually break down the rock into small pieces called sediments. Water and wind carry the sediments down from the mountains.

The Legend of Ural

Legend has it that a great man named Ural lived in Russia in the 13th century. Ural was known for his superhuman strength and courage. He tamed a wild bull with his bare hands, defeated an evil six-headed monster, and rode a winged horse. Ural died when he drank all the water from a lake to remove the demons from it. People piled rocks on Ural's grave to honor him and, over time, the rocks formed the Ural Mountains. Today, the Urals carry the name of the legendary hero.

The Manpupuner rock formations are listed as one of the Seven Wonders of Russia.

Russian Rock Group

Erosion has created many interesting rock formations, or shapes, in the Ural Mountains. Some of the most amazing shapes are found in the Manpupuner rock formations. Manpupuner is a group of gigantic stone pillars on a **plateau** in the Northern Urals. The huge rocks are also called the "Seven Strong Men" or "Seven Brothers" because they look like a group of giants standing together. A local legend tells that the Manpupuner rock formations were created when a group of evil giants were magically turned to stone.

The Ob River is the seventh longest river in the world. It runs north to south on the eastern side of the Urals.

Northern Rivers

There are thousands of rivers in the Ural Mountains. The rivers have shaped the Urals over time, carving deep valleys in the slopes of the mountains. Rivers in the northern parts of the Urals flow into the Arctic Ocean. The Pechora River basin drains the western side of the slopes. Its **tributaries** include the Ilych, Shchugor, and Usa rivers. The Ob River basin drains the eastern side of the slopes. It is fed by the Tobol, Tavda, Iset, Tura, Lyapin, and Severnaya Sosva rivers.

Southern Rivers

Rivers in the southern parts of the Urals drain into the Caspian Sea. The Kama and Ural rivers are the main drainage basins. The Kama River is fed by many tributaries, including the Vishera, Chusovaya, and Belaya rivers. The Ural River is fed by the Sakmara. Rivers in the southern areas flow slower and have less water than northern rivers because there is less snow in this area. When snow melts, it fills rivers with cold, fresh water.

After the Volga and Danube rivers, the Ural River is the third longest river in Europe.

The Belaya River is 889 miles (1,430 km) long.

Lots of Lakes

There are also many lakes in the Ural Mountains. Most of the deep lakes, including the Uvildy, Itkul, Turgoyak, and Tavatuy, are found on the eastern side of the mountains in the Central and Southern Urals. There are lakes on the western side of the mountains, too, but they are fewer and smaller. There are also glacial lakes in the Polar Urals. Glacial lakes are formed when **glaciers** move down a mountain, carving deep holes in the land. The glaciers melt and fill with water, creating lakes.

The clear waters of Lake Turgoyak attract countless tourists each year.

The Gofman glacier in Sabre Mountain has created pools of meltwater, which are glacial lakes.

Western Rocks and Caves

The Ural Mountains are narrow compared to some mountain ranges, stretching only about 20 to 90 miles (32 to 145 km) across. The **geology** of the slopes varies from east to west, however. The western side of the Ural Mountains is made up mostly of **sedimentary rocks**, including limestone and sandstone. Limestone is partly soluble, which means that it can be dissolved, or turned into liquid. Where the limestone has been dissolved on the western Urals, there are ridges, towers, and other rock formations, small caves, and large caves called caverns. There are also many underground streams.

Kungur Ice Cave

The Kungur Ice Cave is one of the longest caves of its kind in the world and one of the biggest tourist attractions in the Urals. The cave stretches 3.5 miles (5.7 km) through the western slopes of the mountains. It is a maze of small caves, passageways, and sparkling underground lakes. The Kungur Ice Cave is most famous, however, for the beauty and variety of its ice formations. There are more than 120 different kinds of ice formations inside the cave, including ice crystals, columns, arches, and huge icicles called stalactites.

Eastern Foothills and Buttes

On the eastern side of the mountains, the land is rocky but flatter than the western side. There are wide **foothills** in the Central and Southern Urals. There are also many buttes, or large, flat rocks with steep sides. Buttes form when a more resistant layer of rock covers and protects less resistant rock below it. A rock that is resistant is not as affected or changed by weather and water as other rocks are. The eastern slopes of the Ural Mountains are made up of both sedimentary and igneous rocks. Igneous rocks are formed when hot melted rock cools and hardens. Igneous rocks are more resistant than sedimentary rocks.

This butte rises high above a forest in the Urals.

Hard Rock

Most of the highest peaks in the Ural Mountains are made up of metamorphic rocks such as quartzite and slate. Metamorphic rocks are the hardest and most resistant rocks on Earth. They are formed when extreme heat and pressure act on existing rocks. The metamorphic rocks in the Urals have stood up to hundreds of millions of years of extreme Russian weather—and have come out on top.

Quartz is exposed in rock at Zyuratkul National Park in Russia.

CHAPTER 3

Changing Weather

The climate of the Ural Mountains is continental. A continental climate has weather that is very different at different times of the year. Temperatures in the Ural Mountains change from season to season and can be extreme. The climate of the mountains also varies from north to south and from east to west. It is different on the bottom of the mountains than it is on the top of the mountains, too. The climate of the Urals varies because the mountains affect the temperature, wind, **precipitation**, and other aspects of the weather.

The Northern Urals endure bitter winters characterized by snow and freezing temperatures.

Snow in the Nether-Polar and Northern Urals can average 35 inches (89 cm) deep.

Cooler at the Top

Like all mountains, the Ural Mountains are colder at the top than they are at the bottom. In general, the temperature falls about one degree for every 300 feet (100 m) of **altitude**. The temperature drops because there is less gravity at higher altitudes, which makes the air thinner. Thinner air holds less heat and makes the temperatures colder. Some peaks of the Urals are covered with snow and ice all year long. Lower on the mountains, the weather changes from season to season.

Long, Cold Winters

Winters in the Urals are long, lasting for about seven months of the year. They often bring severe weather to the region. In the northern areas of the mountains, the weather is bitterly cold and snowy. Temperatures can drop as low as -76° F (-60° C). In the south, winters are cold and dry. There is not a lot of snow to cover and protect the ground, so the soil often freezes. Since the snowfall is light, it blows around and can create **blizzard** conditions.

In the coldest parts of Russia, such as the Siberian tundra, permafrost can be as thick as 1,968 feet (600m).

The Frozen North

In the Polar and Nether-Polar Urals, almost everything is frozen! **Permafrost** covers much of the land. There are also more than 140 glaciers in the northern areas.

Boating and rafting are popular activities for tourists in the summer on the Chusovaya River.

Short, Warm Summers

Summers in the Ural Mountains are short, lasting for only a couple of months each year. The warmest months are July and August. In the southern areas, the weather is hot. Temperatures can reach as high as 104° F (40° C)! The climate is also very dry. Some parts of the Southern Urals are **semideserts**. Summer temperatures in the northern areas of the Ural Mountains are much cooler. The temperatures are also cooler higher in the mountains.

Russia is one of the world's largest producers of sunflower seeds.

Wind Barrier

The climate is also different on the eastern and western slopes of the mountains because the mountains act as a wind barrier. Although the Urals are not as high as some other mountains, they block much of the wind that blows across Russia. During the winter, the mountains protect the western slopes from the cold air that blows in from Siberia. The Siberian High is a massive area of cold, dry air that collects east of the Ural Mountains for much of the year. It is largest and most powerful in winter, when it creates record-breaking low temperatures. The Siberian High brings biting winds to the eastern slopes of the Urals each winter, making them colder than the western slopes of the mountains.

Rain Shadow

The Urals also block the eastern slopes of the mountains from westerly winds. Westerly winds blow in from the west and are the **prevailing winds** of the Urals. Westerly winds carry precipitation from the Atlantic Ocean, which is located far west of the Ural Mountains. The western slopes get 20 to 40 inches (50 to 100 cm) of rain each year, with the most rain falling in the Nether-Polar and Northern Urals during the summer months. The eastern slopes of the mountains get much less rain. They are in a **rain shadow**. The eastern slopes of the Urals get only about 12 to 19 inches (30 to 48 cm) of rain each year. The western slopes of the mountains also get about twice as much snow as the eastern slopes.

CHAPTER 4

Plants and Animals

Many animals make their homes on the slopes of the Ural Mountains. Since the mountains are relatively low, it is easy for animals to climb them. In fact, the same species, or kinds, of animals live in the Ural Mountains as in nearby areas of eastern Europe and western Siberia. Many species of plants grow in the Urals, too. The species are well suited to the diverse **biomes** found in the long mountain range. Different species live in different biomes of the Ural Mountains.

Reindeer have two layers of warm fur. A dense, woolly undercoat and a long, hairy outer layer protect reindeer from cold winter temperatures.

Shrubby birch and fir trees grow in sparse forests in the tundra.

Polar Plants

Although plants grow throughout the Ural Mountains, few species can survive in the harsh tundra. The tundra is a biome that has very low temperatures, short growing seasons, and frozen ground. It is found in the Polar and Nether-Polar Urals and in high altitudes in other parts of the mountain range. The soil in the tundra is frozen all winter. In summer, only the top layer of soil above the permafrost thaws. Hardy plants with shallow roots grow in the thin layer of soil. The plants grow close to the ground to avoid the strong northern winds. Low trees, shrubs, grasses, mosses, and lichens grow in the harsh conditions of the tundra. Berries, including blueberries, cloudberries, and black crowberries, also grow there.

Lonely at the Top

Few animals can survive in the freezing tundra. The animals that do live there—including arctic foxes, reindeer, and small rodents called lemmings—are well suited to their habitats. They have all **adapted** in different ways to survive the extreme cold. Arctic foxes have deep, thick fur, even on the bottoms of their paws. Their fur changes color in the seasons for camouflage. It is white during the snowy winter months and brown during the summer. Lemmings burrow under the snow to keep warm, find food, and hide from predators.

The Arctic fox's thick fur and good supply of body fat help it to adapt to the extreme cold of the tundra.

The Tree Line

The tree line is the highest point on a mountain where trees can grow. No trees grow above the tree line on the top of mountains because the climate is too harsh for them to survive. In most areas of the Ural Mountains, the tree line is about 3,280 feet (1,000 m) above the ground. In the Polar Urals, however, the tree line is only 820 to 1,310 feet (250 to 400 m) above the ground. The tree line is lower in the northern part of the Ural Mountains because the temperatures are much colder there.

Larch and conifer forests grow in the taiga of the Urals.

Northern Conifers

South of the tundra in the Northern Urals, trees grow in a biome called the taiga. The taiga is also known as a boreal forest. It is a huge forest made up mostly of coniferous trees. Coniferous trees, or conifers, have cones and needle-shaped leaves. Several species of coniferous trees, including Siberian pine, Scots pine, Siberian fir, Siberian spruce, Norway spruce, and Siberian larch, grow in the Northern Urals. The trees grow in immense, thick forests.

The Virgin Komi Forests

The Virgin Komi Forests is a vast area of coniferous trees in the Northern Urals. It is the largest old-growth forest in Europe. Old-growth forests are ancient forests with special features. They are often home to rare species of animals. The Virgin Komi Forests was named a UNESCO World Heritage Site in 1995. It was the first natural site to receive the honor in Russia.

Central Mixed Forests

The Central Urals are made up of mixed forests. Mixed forests contain both coniferous and broadleaved trees. Broadleaved trees have leaves that are wide and flat. The trees grow leaves in the warm weather and then lose their leaves when the weather turns cold. In this part of the Urals, broadleaved trees such as elm, English oak, and Norway maple grow alongside fir, pine, and other conifers.

Down the Southern Steppes

Broadleaved and coniferous trees grow in different parts of the Southern Urals. The low mountains in this area also roll into **steppes**. In the lower parts of the mountain slopes, steppes are covered with mountain clovers, dropwort, and meadow grasses. Higher up the mountains, the steppes are rockier and fewer plants grow. In the southernmost part of the Urals near the Mughalzhar Hills, the land is very dry. There are fewer meadows and plants in this semidesert area of the Urals.

The southern steppes are home to many burrowing animals such as hares, gophers, and jerboas.

NOTABLE QUOTE

"Let us learn to appreciate there will be times when the trees will be bare, and look forward to the time when we may pick the fruit."

—Russian writer Anton Chekhov

Forest Habitats

Animals of all kinds live in the thick forest habitats of the Ural Mountains. The forests provide shelter and plenty of food for brown bears, elk and other deer, foxes, and lynx. Smaller mammals, such as wolverines, martens, weasels, and squirrels, also live there. Many species of birds, including wood grouse and cuckoos, nest in the forests year round. Songbirds visit the forests in the warm summer months. When the weather begins to turn cold, they **migrate** to warmer climates.

The white winter feathers of many northern birds, including the Snowy Owl and Rock Ptarmigan, allow them to blend in with the snowy tundra.

Many fish live in rivers and lakes in the Urals providing food for other animals, such as this brown bear. Common species include whitefish, salmon, grayling, and sea trout.

Wood grouse live in coniferous forests in the Ural Mountains. In winter, the birds eat the needles of the trees. They are one of the few species in the world that has adapted to eat the sharp needles.

Stepping Home

There are fewer animals in the Central and Southern Urals than in other areas of the mountains because more people live there. Houses and factories have replaced the natural habitats of much of the wildlife in the regions. In the grassy steppes and semidesert areas of the Southern Urals, the most common animals are hares and rodents such as gophers and ground squirrels. Reptiles such as lizards and snakes also live in this part of the mountains. The small animals provide food for birds of prey that fly in southern skies.

The suslik, which means "seed-lover" in Russian, is a ground squirrel that lives in open areas barren of trees.

CHAPTER 5

Homes on the Range

People have lived in the Ural Mountains for a very long time. The first settlements were built at the start of the Middle Stone Age, about 75 thousand years ago. Ancient tribes from the continents of Europe and Asia lived on the slopes of the Ural Mountains on opposite sides. The tribes crossed the mountains to hunt and eventually shared their cultures and learned from one another.

The Komi peoples live along the Pechora River in northwest Russia.

Ancient Tribes

Most ancient tribes were nomadic, which means they were always traveling through the mountains. Some tribes settled in the Urals, where they hunted and fished for food. They grew crops and raised cattle on the land. Today, indigenous people make up about one-fifth of the population of the Ural Mountains. They speak native languages and maintain the traditional ways of their tribes. Tribes such as the Nenets and Komi live high in the mountains in even the cold northern parts of the Urals. There, they hunt and gather food, fish in mountain lakes and rivers, and raise reindeer. The Bashkir live in the warmer Southern Urals. They breed horses and other cattle, keep bees, and grow crops on the steppes of the mountains.

Cave Paintings

Ancient people sometimes recorded their histories in cave paintings. In the Ural Mountains, the most famous paintings are found in Kapova Cave in the Southern Urals. Scientists believe the drawings were made in the Late Stone Age, about 14,000 years ago. The early paintings stretch more than a mile (1.6 km) through the mountains and include pictures of rhinoceroses, horses, and mammoths. Mammoths are elephant-like animals that no longer live on Earth.

Ancient paintings in the Kapova Cave feature many kinds of animals.

Nenets live in tents called chums.

Arkaim

An archaeological site called Arkaim was discovered in the Southern Urals in 1987. The site dates back to at least 17th century B.C. A team of Russian scientists found Arkaim by accident when they were preparing to build a **reservoir**. Although the ancient settlement had been abandoned and burned long ago, many details of Arkaim were preserved. Scientists discovered buildings and streets organized within two thick circular walls. They also found furnaces, a water system, fields, and mines. Today, many local Russians believe that Arkaim is a **sacred** place. They visit the ancient site because they think it has special healing powers. Arkaim is often compared to Stonehenge—a prehistoric circular stone monument in the United Kingdom. No one is really sure what the purpose of either site was intended to be.

This home from the Stone Age has been reconstructed at the Arkaim site.

NOTABLE QUOTE

"Architecture is also a chronicle of the world: it still speaks out when all songs and legends fall silent, and when already nothing else points to the perished people."

—Russian writer Nikolai Gogol

Finding and Founding the Urals

Russians discovered the northernmost area of the Ural Mountains at the end of the 11th century. By the start of the 1600s, they had discovered the entire mountain range. In the early 1700s, Russians began to explore and settle the land under the command of Tsar Peter the Great, who wanted to expand his empire. A geographer named Vasily Tatishchev **surveyed** the mountain range for the tsar. Tatishchev founded the cities of Perm and Yekaterinburg in the Ural Mountains in 1723. He also managed the new factories in the region's growing cities.

Tatishchev was born near the ancient city of Pskov in Russia in 1686.

Relying on Resources

In the 1930s, Russians built many factories in the Ural Mountains. They built factories there because the Urals had a lot of **minerals** and other natural resources they needed. For example, the Magnitaya mountain in the Southern Urals was made up almost entirely of iron. Russians built a huge iron and steel plant near the mountain. A town called Magnitogorsk grew around the factory. Today, Magnitogorsk is a busy industrial city that continues to depend on the natural resources in the area.

This monument is a tribute to the steelworkers of Magnitogorsk that work in the city's huge steel plant. The factory is one of the leading producers of steel in the world.

The Leaning Tower of Nevyansk is a building in the Urals that was made with advanced metalworking techniques around 1725.

Big Business

Factory workers in the 1930s made heavy machines that were used for mining and metallurgy. Metallurgy is the science of getting metals from rocks and changing them to a form that can be used to produce goods. During World War II, Russians also moved hundreds of factories from Moscow and other western cities to the Central and Southern Urals. They moved the factories far from the borders of other countries so they would not be destroyed in the war. Russians built many more factories in the Urals after the war ended. The region became a major manufacturing center for the country.

The Trans-Siberian Railway is the longest railway in the world. It passes through the Ural Mountains on its eight-day journey across Russia.

Passing Through

Since the Urals are not high mountains, it is fairly easy for people to travel through them. There are several low passes through the range. Passes are routes or paths built over or through mountains. Passes in the Ural Mountains allow workers to transport goods to and from factories. They also allow Russians and tourists to travel through the Urals by car, bus, or train.

Busy Cities

Today, most people live and work in busy industrial cities in the Central and Southern Urals. Yekaterinburg, Chelyabinsk, Ufa, Perm, Magnitogorsk, Nizhny Tagil, and Orsk are the biggest cities in and around the mountains. Many people live in the cities and work in factories there. Factory workers in the Urals produce iron, steel and other metals, machines, cars, chemicals, and many other goods. They buy some of the products themselves and ship the rest to other parts of Russia and other countries around the world.

FAST FACT

Doctor Zhivago is one of the most famous Russian novels ever written. The fictional town in the book is based on the city of Perm in the Urals.

This bridge spans the Ural River and joins the city of Orsk together—one side in Asia, the other in Europe.

(above) The city of Perm is intersected by three main transportation routes—the Kama River, the Trans-Siberian Railway, and highways from Moscow to Siberia.

(left) Oil refining is one of the largest industries in Ufa, one of Russia's largest cities.

Yekaterinburg Rocks!

Yekaterinburg is the largest city in the Ural Mountains and the fourth-largest city in Russia. More than 1.3 million people live there. It is a major industrial center for the entire country. There is more to the city than just industry. Yekaterinburg is also famous for its culture, including its theaters, museums, dance, and music. Many popular Russian rock bands started there. They made "Ural Rock," a kind of Russian rock music, popular throughout the country in the 1980s and 90s.

The Opera and Ballet House in Yekaterinburg is one of Russia's oldest cultural centers.

(Above) Vyacheslav Butusov was lead singer in the band Nautilus Pompilius.

Steppe Farming

Many Russians also farm in the Southern Urals. The steppes on the eastern side of the mountains are good for growing crops. Farmers plow large areas of land for agriculture, or farming. They grow wheat, potatoes, buckwheat, millet, vegetables, and other crops there.

a potato field

Showing Their Metal

Hockey is extremely popular. The are several professional hockey teams in Russia, including Metallurg Magnitogorsk. Popular players Evgeni Malkin and Nikolai Kulemin grew up in and played for Magnitogorsk. Both went on to play in the National Hockey League in North America.

Nikolai Kulemin

Evgeni Malkin

NOTABLE QUOTE

"I can't but recall the old wooden house where I spent my early childhood years. At least one remarkable thing about it was that one of its sides faced Europe and the opposite side—Asia. I could see both continents from its windows…"

—Russian writer Dmitry Mamin-Sibiryak, who grew up in the Urals

CHAPTER 6

Rich in Resources

What the Ural Mountains lack in height, they make up for in natural resources. The Urals are extremely rich in resources of all kinds. The rocks and minerals, bodies of water, and vast forests of the Urals are very important to people who live in the mountains and throughout Russia.

Quarries, which are open-pit mines from which rocks and minerals are taken, can be found throughout the Urals.

Mining the Mountains

In the 1600s, Russians discovered that the Urals were rich in high-quality minerals and ore. Ore is rock that contains valuable minerals or metals. People began mining the mountains in the 1700s. Miners dug deep in the ground to find and get iron and copper ore. Then they smelted the ore. Smelting is a process in which rock is heated so the metal can be removed from it.

Mountains of Minerals and Metals

Today, the Ural Mountains have a greater amount and variety of minerals than most other places in the world. There are nearly 50 types of minerals and ores in the Urals that are very important for mining. Some of the minerals that are mined in the Urals are magnetite, chromite, and talc. Valuable metal ores, such as iron, copper, nickel, chromium, aluminum, gold, and platinum are found in the mountains. Coal, oil, and natural gas are also extracted there.

Copper is mined for many uses, including in electrical wires, roofing and plumbing, and for making jewelry.

Marble blocks are extracted from this mine in Chelyabinsk, in Russia.

Mapping the Mountains

In 1841, a Scottish scientist named Sir Roderick Murchison made the first geological map of the Ural Mountains. A geological map shows the age, type, and features of rocks and minerals in a certain area. The map helped people effectively mine the mountains.

In 2005, a stone memorial tablet was installed in front of a school in Perm. It reads: To Roderick Impey Murchison, Scottish geologist, explorer of Perm Krai, who gives to the last period of Paleozoic era the name of Perm.

Garnet

What a Gem!

Many precious gems are mined in the Ural Mountains. Gems are pieces of minerals that are prized for their beautiful colors and shine. Diamonds, emeralds, amethysts, topaz, and garnet are some of the gems found in the Ural Mountains. The gems are cut and polished and used to make jewelry of all kinds.

N O T A B L E   Q U O T E

"Although I have seen numbers of deposits of semiprecious stones before… nowhere was I so deeply impressed by the richness and beauty of nature as at the Urals excavation sites."

—Russian mineralogist Alexander Fersman

Poisonous Pollution

Although the resources of the Ural Mountains are good for Russians, the way people use the resources is not always good for the Ural Mountains. Mining and manufacturing cause a lot of pollution in the area. They produce lead, sulfur dioxide, and other dangerous pollutants. Pollutants poison the air, water, and soil, and hurt all living things in the Ural Mountains.

Radioactive Rivers

Russians began secretly producing plutonium in the Southern Urals in 1949. Plutonium is a dangerous **radioactive** metal that is used to make nuclear weapons. In the first ten years of production, workers dumped huge amounts of radioactive waste into the Techa River, Lake Karachay, and other nearby waters. In 1957, the "Kyshtym disaster" took place at the plutonium plant. The factory, called Mayak, released large amounts of radioactive waste into the air. Huge areas of land around the plant were contaminated, or poisoned. Thousands of people in that part of the Ural Mountains have died or are now very sick because of the factory's deadly pollution.

The air, water, and soil pollution in Karabash, a copper-smelting town, has earned it the name "most polluted" town in Russia.

Water Power

Water is another very important resource in the Ural Mountains. Lakes and rivers in the range provide fresh water for people and animals to drink and for farmers to water their crops. The lakes and rivers also enable workers to transport goods to and from their factories.

Water is also used to provide power to the people of the Urals. **Hydroelectric** dams on the rivers produce electricity so people can light and heat their homes. The dams also help create reservoirs, which store water for drinking, transportation, and scientific studies. Some examples are the Kama Reservoir and Votkinsk Reservoir.

In the city of Satka, in Chelyabinsk Oblast, Russia, the first hydroelectric generator in Russia was installed. It is still running today.

Timber!

The vast forests of the Northern and Central Urals are a valuable resource for Russia. The forests provide much of the country's timber supply. Timber is wooden boards that are used for building and carpentry. People use timber to make homes, furniture, and many other wooden items. The thick forests of the Ural Mountains also provide homes and shelter for many animals. Russians hunt and trap the animals and sell their fur to earn money.

Russian forests are at risk because they regrow at a very slow rate after being cut down due to the cold climate.

This church in a theme park on Lake Zyuratkul is made entirely of wood.

Disappearing Forests

Clearing is a problem in some wooded parts of the Urals. Clearing is cutting down and removing all the trees and other plants from an area. People clear forests so they can sell the logs or make room for towns and roads. Clearing has destroyed some important old-growth forests in the Ural Mountains. It has also left some species of animals without their natural habitats. When animals lose their habitats, it is very difficult for them to make homes and find food.

Animals in Danger

Some species of animals in the Ural Mountains are endangered, or at risk of dying out forever. The animals are endangered because they have lost their habitats or because too many of them have been hunted. Wild reindeer were once common in some parts of the Urals. Their pine forest habitats were destroyed and they are now in danger of dying out. Other animals, such as the Lesser Kestrel and Eastern Imperial Eagle, are also at risk of disappearing from the Ural Mountains forever.

Bringing Back the Beavers

European Beavers were once common in the Ural Mountains. In the 1600s and 1700s, Russians hunted the animals for their valuable furs. They also hunted them for their scent glands, which were used to make medicines. By the 1800s, European Beavers had become extinct in the region, which means that the species of animal no longer existed there. In 1949, **conservationists** successfully reintroduced European Beavers to the Ural Mountains. To reintroduce is to release a species into a wild area where it once lived. Today, beavers are common in the mountains once again.

This aspen tree has been nearly chewed through by the gnawing of a beaver.

The Eastern Imperial Eagle is a large migratory bird that is threatened with extinction.

Nature Reserves

To help protect plant and animal species in the Urals, the Russian government has turned some wildlife areas into nature reserves. Nature reserves are protected areas of land where people are not allowed to hunt animals or destroy trees or other plants. There are several nature reserves throughout the Urals, including Basegi Nature Reserve in the Central Urals and Ilmen Nature Reserve in the Southern Urals. Vishera Nature Reserve in the Northern Urals is one of the largest nature reserves in Europe. With an area of 931 square miles (2,412 sq km), Vishera is nearly as big as the country of Luxembourg. The reserve is home to many wildlife species, including brown bears and reindeer.

Adding Russia's Virgin Komi Forests to UNESCO's list of World Heritage Sites in 1995 has helped protect the nature reserves contained within them from illegal logging and gold mining.

National Parks

There are also several national parks in the Ural Mountains. Like nature reserves, national parks are protected areas of land. Tourism and recreation are, however, allowed in the parks. Thousands of adventurous tourists visit Yugyd Va National Park in the Northern Urals each year. It is the largest park in the Ural Mountains. It is also the biggest national park in both Russia and Europe. The huge park covers 7,300 square miles (18,917 sq km) of land. Some 180 species of birds and 20 species of fish live in the park, as well as moose, wolves, foxes, and many other animals.

There are many sparkling rivers and lakes in Yugyd Va National Park. The park's name means "clear water."

People come from all over the world to hike in the Ural Mountains.

Exploring the Mountains

The Ural Mountains are a paradise for nature lovers. Many tourists visit the Urals each year, particularly in the warmer summer months. The most popular areas for active vacations are the unspoiled Northern and Nether-Polar Urals. In the summer, tourists go boating, rafting, hiking, and horseback riding there. In the winter, they go skiing and snowboarding on the snowy slopes. Expeditions to mountain caves and summits are also popular adventures in the area. However visitors choose to explore the highs and lows of Russia's gracefully aging mountains, they will not be disappointed by the rugged beauty and natural wonders of the Urals.

TIMELINE

About 300 million years ago	The Ural Mountains are formed when the tectonic plates of Europe and Asia collide. The plates push up and fold the land into mountains.
75,000 years ago	The first settlements are built in the Urals at the start of the Middle Stone Age.
14,000 years ago	Ancient people create paintings in Kapova Cave in the Southern Urals. The drawings show horses, mammoths, and other animals that lived then.
1000s	Russians discover the northernmost area of the Ural Mountains at the end of the 11th century.
1600s	Russians discover the rest of the mountain range. They also discover that the Urals are rich in valuable minerals and ore.
1700s	Russians begin to explore and settle the Ural Mountains under the command of Tsar Peter the Great, who wishes to expand his empire. They also begin mining iron and copper ore in the mountains.
1723	Russian geographer Vasily Tatishchev establishes the cities of Perm and Yekaterinburg and manages their new factories.
1841	A Scottish scientist named Sir Roderick Murchison makes the first geological map of the Ural Mountains.
1916	Construction of the Trans-Siberian Railway is completed. The railway crosses through the Ural Mountains as it connects Moscow to the eastern part of Russia.
1927	An expedition of scientists discovers Mount Narodnaya, the tallest peak in the Urals.
1930s	Russians build many factories in the Ural Mountains because the area has the natural resources they need.
1939–1945	During World War II, workers move hundreds of factories from Moscow and other cities to the Central and Southern Urals so they will not be destroyed. Once the war ends, Russians build many more factories in the Urals.
1949	Conservationists successfully reintroduce European beavers to the Ural Mountains. The beavers had been hunted to extinction in the region.
1949	Russians begin secretly producing plutonium in the Southern Urals. Eight years later, the "Kyshtym disaster" occurs at the Mayak plant. It is the third-worst nuclear accident in history.
1987	Russian scientists accidentally discover the archaeological site Arkaim in the Southern Urals. The well-preserved settlement dates back to at least 17th century B.C. and includes buildings, streets, and mines.
1995	The Virgin Komi Forests area is named a UNESCO World Heritage Site. It becomes the first natural site to receive the honor in Russia.

GLOSSARY

adapt To physically change over time in order to survive in a certain habitat

altitude The height of an object above sea level

biome A large natural area where certain types of plants and animals live

blizzard A windy winter storm with swirling snow

conservationist A person who works to protect and preserve animals and their natural habitats

erosion A natural process in which land is gradually worn away and moved to a new place

foothills Low hills found at the bases of mountains

geographer A person who studies the physical features of Earth and how human activity affects and is affected by the land

geology The type and features of rocks found in a certain area

glacier A huge frozen river that moves slowly down a mountain

hydroelectric Describing electricity that is made by using the movement of rushing water

indigenous Living or occurring naturally in a certain place

migrate To move from one region to another to find food, shelter, or better weather

mineral A solid chemical substance found in the ground

natural resource Something found in nature that people can use

permafrost A layer of ground that stays frozen year round

plateau An area of level high ground

precipitation Rain, snow, hail, or other form of water that falls to the ground

prevailing winds Describing the winds that usually blow from a certain direction

radioactive Describing a substance that gives off dangerous high-energy particles

rain shadow An area of land that is sheltered from precipitation by a large hill or mountain

reservoir An artificial lake where water is collected and stored for use

sacred Describing something that is respected for its special meaning or importance

sedimentary rocks A type of rock formed by layers of sediment that are pressed together over time

semidesert An area of land that receives little precipitation

steppe A large area of flat, grassy meadows found mostly on the eastern side of the mountains

summit The highest point on a mountain

survey To examine and record the features of an area of land to make a map or plan

tributary A smaller river or stream that flows into a larger body of water

uplands An area of hilly or high land

INDEX

FIND OUT MORE

BOOKS

Kalman, Bobbie. *Looking at Earth: Earth's Mountains.* Crabtree Publishing Company, 2009.

Maynard, Charles W. *Great Mountain Ranges of the World: The Ural Mountains*. PowerKids Press, 2004.

Somervill, Barbara A. *Geography of the World: The Timeworn Urals.* Child's World, 2004.

WEBSITES

All Russia Encyclopedia: The Urals

ftp://ftp.vor.ru/input/Burenkov/Encyclopedia_%283%29/6_Ural/%285%29_Ural_EN/EN_Ural_REDY.pdf

Encyclopedia Britannica: Ural Mountains

www.britannica.com/EBchecked/topic/619028/Ural-Mountains

World Wildlife Fund: Ural Mountains Taiga

http://wwf.panda.org/about_our_earth/ecoregions/ural_mountains_taiga.cfm